THE GIRL
WITH A HAPPY HEART

(A journey towards infinite happiness)

Poetry by - Madhuri Gupta

Edited by - Prashant Gupta

Formatted by - Madhusudan Mishra

THE GIRL WITH A HAPPY HEART
(A journey towards infinite happiness)
Copyright © (2025)
Madhuri Gupta

Made with ❤ on the Notion Press Platform
www.notionpress.com

Connect with an Author -   Instagram :- infiiniite_happiness_
E-mail :- writermadhuriofficial@gmail.com

Life shows us lots of ups and down

Sometimes our pinkish sky turned out brown

Yet out of all outer conflicts, don't stress for a while

Your blissful heart always produces a glowing smile

(Madhuri)

ACKNOWLEDGEMENT

To my parents, thank you for reading nearly every page of just about everything I've ever written. This book would not have been completed without you. You're my biggest fan, and I am yours. Bade Papa and Badi Mummy, thank you for showering unconditional love, for sharing your story, and for inspiring me to consider a new idea

To my brothers Prashant, Alok , Anoop, and Maahir and my sisters Anita, Manshi, Maahi, thank you for supporting me in every step of my life, your support care and love motivate me in every step of this book.

To my maternal grandfather (Nana), maternal grandmother (Nani), my aunties (Maasi) thanks for your blessings and love.

A special thanks to my best friend cum sister Ankita for always supporting me and encouraging me

I just wanted to say thanks to my brothers Raj, Shashi Kant Sharma, Komal, Anas. Your support and guidance have meant the world to me, and I'm so grateful for the bond we share, even though we're not blood-related. You're like a brother to me.

To my closest friends Priya, Ruchi, Shrestha, Pratibha Mishra, Sweta, Diksha , Manisha, Sneha, Rupal, Vijayata, Jahanavi, I just wanted to say thank you for being such a great friend. You all always know how to make me smile.

A big thanks to Mr. Madhusudan Mishra sir, I am incredibly grateful for your help with my books; your support and guidance made a real difference. Thanks to my colleagues for always supporting me in my thick and thins.

To my school head Reena Ma'am and my teachers, thank you for helping me discover what I'm good at and always encouraging me to do my best 'My school Gyan Peethika Senior Secondary School set grounding for my success', 'My school forbade to inculcate values in me, such as discipline and empathy.

A huge bunch of thanks to the dearest eye who decided to pick this book and read my thoughts. Thanks to technology "artificial intelligence" that helps me in creating images .

Finally, I would like to thank God, I am extremely grateful for all of your blessings in my life.

Ballia, Uttar Pradesh
30 March 2025

ABOUT THE AUTHOR

Madhuri Gupta, a chemistry lecturer from Ballia, Uttar Pradesh, wears many hats - teacher, poet, and mental health advocate. Her journey as a poet began as a cathartic expression of her own struggles and triumphs with mental health.

Through her poetry, Madhuri seeks to normalize conversations around mental wellness, encouraging readers to prioritize self-care, self-love, and happiness. Her words are a testament to the transformative power of vulnerability, resilience, and hope.

As a chemistry lecturer, Madhuri has learned to balance the precision of science with the creativity of art. Her poetry reflects this unique blend, offering readers a nuanced exploration of the human experience.

Apart from writing, she loves to sing and listen to music. She wants to spread happiness and positivity. She believes in the quote of Mother Teresa-"Spread love everywhere you golet no one come to you without leaving happier".

In this collection, Madhuri invites readers to embark on a journey of self-discovery, healing, and growth. May her words be a beacon of light, guiding you toward a brighter, happier you.

Connect with the Author - *Instagram :-infiiniite_happiness_*
E-mail :-writermadhuriofficial@gmail.com

Contents

FRIENDLY REMINDER

When your heart is full of childness
You see everyday a new miracle of joyness

SMILE, SMILE AND SMILE

Smile like an innocent child
Magical, pure and kind
Who only know to laugh
No matter moon is full or half

Smile like an angelic star
That is twinkling so far
Who only knows to shine bright
No matter sky is blue or white

Smile like a blooming flower
Holding pearl of cheerful colour
Who only knows to glow
No matter bluish wind is fast or slow

Smile like a reddish dawn
Wearing rays of a golden crown
Who only knows to rise
No matter world is silent or full of noise

Smile like a blissful rain
Wiping away all the sadness and pain
Who only knows to celebrate happiness
No matter day is hard or full of joyness

Smile like an innocent child
Magical, pure and kind

FRIENDLY REMINDER

The beauty of you lies in
How boldly you rise after every fall
How beautifully you shine in darker night
How perfectly you walk in a harder way
How calmly you Smile everyday
Buddies you're the epitome of true beauty

A MESSAGE TO THE BEAUTIFUL PEOPLE

To the girl who think they are not pretty
Who compared in other eyes about her identity
Darling stop doubting your beauty
You are as charming as New York City

To the boy who always suffers to try
To fit in societal law 'Men don't cry'
Dude please don't be so so shy
You are as brave as Murad of Gully Boy

To the one who feel shame of their body shape
Who think they have no happy scope
Buddy keeps the sadness so so far
You are as sweet as milky bar

To the one who hates their skin tone
Who think they are worthless like stone
Buddy don't be so so sad
You are as precious as a glowing diamond

To everyone who feels low about their looks and weight
Who think they don't fit on society beauty checklist
Trust me you're beautiful just the way you are
You are a cute shining superstar

FRIENDLY REMINDER

And when you're too busy visiting
The back pages of your book
You miss creating everything happy and beautiful
In the new pages lies in front of you

YOU START SMILING AGAIN

Yesterday you wake up with crying eyes
All you see is a darker skies
Your days are not in your favour
You think the pains remains forever

But today you feel a little less pain
Outside it is little less rain
You stood a little taller
You smiled a little wider

Your pain start healing
Your cracks start filling
Your tears start evaporating
Your sadness starts melting

From tomorrow your sky glow more bright
Everywhere you see a happiness light
Your stars again start shining
Your days again start smiling

FRIENDLY REMINDER

Buddies
Never be the version second of someone else
Always be the best version of yourselves

BE THE FIRST RATE VERSION OF YOURSELF

They show us they are perfect
Their life is full of luxury and happiness
But there are always hidden lies and fact
Between those pics and smiling face

Even if they have decorative skies
With lots of money in a saving account
Your life is also good as it is
With millions of blessings in your happiness account

Everyone is different and unique
They like colour light, you prefer colour dark
They look pretty in lipstick pink
You look cute in Kajal black

They are beautiful the way they are
Like a smiling rainbow in reddish noon
You're beautiful the way you are
Like a shining star on the full moon

Never be the carbon copy of someone else
Never try to understand yourself
Because beautiful are those ones
Who never stop loving their authentic self

FRIENDLY REMINDER

Buddies, don't let the dark clouds of fear and loneliness
Dim your pinkish glory of happiness

GOODBYE TO FEAR

Fear of failure will stop you
From construction your dream blue
Fear of being judged surely will
Stop you from learning a new skill

Fear of insecurities will stop you from
Moving out from the four walled room
Fear of society will stop you
From trying something new

Fear of darkness will stop you
From enjoying sunset view
Fear of ignorance will definitely
Stop you from living happily

Fear of being broken
Will stop you from loving again
Fear of dark sobbing sadness
Will stop you from celebrating happiness

Mate be brave, be fearless
Be happy, be stressful
You should move forward without fearing
For you a happy and beautiful future is waiting

FRIENDLY REMINDER

The happiest people you can ever meet is
"you"

EVERYONE IS HAPPY

Happy the moon
Happy the noon
Happy the sky blue
Why not you?

Happy the rain
Happy the singing train
Happy the glowing crystal dew
Why not you?

Happy the flowers
Happy the true lovers
Happy the laughing Pooh
Why not you?

Happy the dawn
Happy the chocolate town
Happy the animal at zoo
Why not you?

Happy the birds
Happy the rhyming words
Happy the smiling rainbow too
Why not you?
Why not you?

FRIENDLY REMINDER

When you fall in love with a right person
Your everyday is like a happy season

90'S LOVE STORY

I like 90's love story
The era which creates an inspiring history
The era when love is connected to the soul
When two lovers complete the world's whole

I like 90's love songs
The songs which connect two lover heart's
The era when Juliet wrote thousands of letters to the
universe
When Romeo starts composing love verse

I like 90's love season
When people love without condition, without reason
The era when love smiles in heart new
When both lover's enjoy watching sunset view

I like 90's love colour
The era when lover shows their love by giving flower
The era when unconditional love gives happiness wing
When every season is like spring

I like 90's love promises
The era when love is a gift, not a business
The era when lover's hold hands for lifetime together
When love comes with the tag of forever

FRIENDLY REMINDER

In this life many can tried to transform your dreams
Into broken pieces of paper
Yet darling no one but yourself
can change it into a beautiful masterpiece

THE BEAUTY OF DREAMS

Dreams fill your bluish emptiness
With the glitter of pinkish happiness
Dreams light up your lonely night
With the sparkles of twinkling starlight

Dreams Paint the canvas of endless scope
With the colours of new hope
Dreams rewrite the empty page
With the charming words of courage

Dreams give you limitless sky to fly
With the inspiring wings of bravery
Dreams decorate your barren world's
With the stars of happy vibes

Dreams vanish away clouds of loneliness
With the golden sunshine of gladness
Dreams add the colour of joyness
With the smiling spoon of childness

Dreams fill your bluish emptiness
With the glitter of pinkish happiness

FRIENDLY REMINDER

Dear Men
Do a universe a little favour
Don't stop being authentic you ever

MEN DO CRY

To all the men of this world's
The one who are like sunshine or the one like happy
word's
I know you all are growing up listening "men don't cry"
Crying makes you a weaker guy

But dude trust me it's a biggest scam
Wrapped in a silvery name of societal fame
You're a human and have an emotional too
Stop listening to others people view

Mate don't be so so sad
Don't think crying sometimes makes you bad
You're most strongest, most handsome guy
You're so so brave dear cutiepie

It's ok to cry when you're feeling unwell
It's ok to cry when you got fail
It's ok to cry when you're not feeling good
It's ok to cry when you're in a bad mood

It's ok to cry when you face breakup
It's ok to cry and never give up
It's ok to cry when you're kept trying and trying
It's ok to cry when you're feeling crying

FRIENDLY REMINDER

Buddies, don't wait for someone to
Motivate you
Supports you or
Complete you
Just look at the mirror and tell yourself
You're perfect and worthy

I WAS CONSTANTLY LOOKING FOR SOMEONE

I was constantly looking at the window
Waiting for sunshine to embrace my shadow
To light up my room and paint my walls
With all the colours of happiness and hopeful smiles

I was constantly looking at the door
Waiting for someone to enter and make me happy more
To hold my hand and introduce me to a laughing world's
With their happy vibes and calming words

I was constantly waiting and waiting and waiting
But unluckily for me, no one is coming
So, I shutdown all the windows and door
And thought in my head, I'm the owner of happiness
store

Because I'm the sunshine and love I'm searching in
other
Only I can fix myself and put all the broken pieces
together
Only I can give peace and calmness to my inner storm
Only I can give strength and make myself feel like a
home

Be your own sunshine, your smiling happiness
Be your own strength, your peaceful calmness
Be your own favourite, your pretty lucky charm
Be your own friend, your playful cute rhyme

FRIENDLY REMINDER

Buddies, always hold the lamp of positivity
To light up your darker bluish sky world

THE BEAUTY OF WAITING

Waiting has shine of its own
like a longing road painted in crimson stone
Like a flightless birds waiting for wing
Like a leafless autumn tree waiting for spring

Waiting is a sign of true love and patience
Like a poet express their feelings by words silence
Like an April noon waiting for the moonlight
Like a darkness waiting for the smiling light

Like a lonely night waiting for a happy day
Like a busy Monday waiting for a chilling Sunday
Like a noisy storm waiting for calmness
I'm waiting for you, my happiness

I know one day we will meet again
Under the blanket of stars in spring rain
With lots of happiness and no pain
And from that day our golden life begin

I hope that, this blissful day come soon
Like after morning there is noon
I wish our love smiles like a silvery full moon
And our cursed life changes into a boon

FRIENDLY REMINDER

Buddies, we all are made of hope, courage, happiness
and everything that smiles

SHE WEAR A CROWN OF HOPE

She wears a golden crown of hope
She dances happily holding the positive rope
She chooses healing over pain
She holds the umbrella of courage in destructive rain

She chooses joyousness over loneliness
She chooses loyalty over faithlessness
She chooses kindness over rudeness
She chooses happiness over sadness

She chooses self-love over a toxic lover
She chooses to be a giver over a taker
She chooses bravery over Fear
She chooses to be a saviour over a survivor

She chooses to be productive over giving up
She chooses to be an authentic over heavy make-up
She chooses to be stronger over the weaker version
She chooses spring over the autumn season

She is a dreamer with millions of dreams in
her eyes
To fly high in the limitless skies
She is real, she has a scar
But still, she shines like a star

FRIENDLY REMINDER

And now Buddies, it's high to say goodbye
To all those people who try to steal your peace of mind

HELLO TO JOYOUSNESS

You are so addicted to pain and suffering
Trying hard to fix the one who always keep hurting
Breaking your own heart again and again
Crying all days and night in the sadness rain

Holding the bond that breaks you from inside
Putting the fake mask of a smile outside
Keep trying to calm the stormy wind
In the process all your happiness end

Now it's high time to say goodbye
To all the toxic one that makes you cry
Say hello to hope, positivity and childness
Let's again be the friend of happiness

Choose the people who feels like sunshine
Choose the people who makes your everyday fine
Choose the people who chooses you
Choose the people who never gonna give up on you

FRIENDLY REMINDER

Buddies, choose to be happy inside
Even if it's stormy outside

I STAY POSITIVE EVERYTIME

I stay positive everytime
Not because I have a charming fame
Not because everything in my life is alright
But because I'm imperfectly perfect
I'm worthy of all good thing
I have a smiling sky and a happiness wing

I stay motivated everytime
Not because I have a famous name
Not because I have a perfect life
But because I'm strong enough
I'm the queen of this golden world's
I have a dreamy eyes and poetic words

I stay happy everytime
Not because my poetry is always rhyme
Not because I have an expensive house and luxury car
But because I never allowed sadness to knock at my
door
I never lose a chance to smiles bright
I have an inspiring stars and hopeful moonlight

I stay positive everytime
I stay happy everytime

FRIENDLY REMINDER

Buddies,
there are far too many silent suffers
kindly when you meet someone give them a flowers of
happiness

WORDS OF SUNSHINE

Words of kindness
Words that bring charming happiness
Words of delight
Words that bring hopeful light

Words of humanity
Words that bring carefree serenity
Words of custom
Words that bring peaceful wisdom

Words, Words, Words
Many more words
Some innocent, some sweet
Some inspiring, some glowing street

Some playing, some dancing
Some verses, some rhyming
Some kind, some healing
Some brave, some calming

Let your words be the healing antiseptic
That heals all the broken heart and painful crack
Let your words be the hopeful light of joyness
For those who lost in the darkness of sadness

FRIENDLY REMINDER

Keep your head up princess
You deserve a crown of colourful happiness

BABY GIRL YOU ARE THE HAPPY SUNSHINE

Baby girl speaks the language of love to you
Fill the colour of happiness in your sky blue
Don't worry about judging society view
You are a shining superstar, kind, innocent and true

Don't let any outer stormy noise
Mute your strong inner voice
Don't let anyone set paths for you to follow
You are an inspiring women of tomorrow

Don't let the clouds of negativity
Dim your pinkish glory of positivity
Don't let some outdated societal norm
Dull your happy glowing charm

So, dares to dream big
And fly high with your bravery wing
Buddy you're a world princess
Treat yourself with love and kindness

Smile and write golden lines in your heart
You are worth it
You are a whole universe
You are always a blessing never a curse

FRIENDLY REMINDER

Buddies,
no one is lonely in this world
God made someone for everyone

WHAT IS LOVE

80 books and 175 love theories
Doesn't explain what love is
It is a tricky magic
Or the road fall of traffic

What is love at first site
Why are people in love talking to moon at night
What happen to all the chemicals in the brain
Why do people behave like a running train

For all these problematic question
I get only one explanation
Which is approved by all the one
That is there is someone for everyone

Evey book has its writer to write
Every song has its singer to sing
Every sun has its sky to glow bright
Every rain has its cloud white

So here all the girl's and boy's
Those who love sunset view or those who like sunrise
Those who talk too much or those who talk less
Those who sing in joyness or those who dance in
happiness

Buddy let's start the journey new
Someone is waiting for me and you
Trust me no one is lonely in the end
Some have lovers, some have a best friend

FRIENDLY REMINDER

You heart is kind and happy
So, show some love and care to yourself kindly
Say bye!! Bye!! to all your pain
Forgive all your past mistake
Remember you don't do it for other self
but for yourself

BE PROUD OF YOURSELF EVERYDAY

Be proud of yourself everyday
For the person you have because today
The person who laughs every single day
The person whose everyday is like a playful Sunday

Do you remember the person you were two years ago
They are so different from who you're now
The person who cried every single night
The person who is afraid to fight for their right

But now you overcome all your stress and fear
You fix the hopeful and happy stars near
You say goodbye to all your worries and sadness
You paint your world in the colour of happiness

In this one year, you worked hard on yourself
Now you grow into the best version of own self
Remember that your superpower lies within you
You're born to shine, and it's one hundred percent true

FRIENDLY REMINDER

Buddies, we all are magician
we have a magical power to hold
the melancholy rain in hand and
turn it into the happiest song

THE SKY OF HER THOUGHT

The sky of her thought
Is pinkish white
Where the moon shines bright
In the twinkling starlight

The floating clouds in the skies
Seems like yellowish butterflies
Where colourful rainbow smiles
In the peaceful moonlights

The laughing rays of positivity
Evaporate the clouds of negativity
Where the star sings a song of happiness
In the dark bluish night of loneliness

Her angelic happy words
Give hope to the hopeless world's
Her blissful pinkish verse
Enlighten the whole universe

FRIENDLY REMINDER

Now Buddies,
it's high time to say goodbye to all your fear, stress and
sadness. It's time to open all windows and welcome the
sunrays
which brings blessing, miracles and happiness in your
life

KNOWING THE REASON OF PAIN

Knowing the reason of pain?
Will you still be sad again?
Or will you try to find pearls of happiness?
Which is lost in the ocean of sadness?

Knowing the reason of stress?
Will you still choose to be depress?
Or will you try to find blissful joyness ?
That is hide behind the clouds of loneliness?

Knowing the reason of worry?
Will you still be in hurry?
Or will you stop for a while?
And find beautiful reason to smile?

Knowing the reason of anger?
Will you still be in danger?
Or will you try to find calmness?
That is lies in the deep sea of humbleness?

Knowing the reason of fear?
Will you still burst out in tear?
Or will you try to find bravery?
That lies in monument of an inspiring history?

Knowing the reason of pain?
Will you still be sad again?

FRIENDLY REMINDER

Buddies,
introduce your strength to your bluish scar
All tell the world
how brave you are

YOU'RE BRAVER THAN YOU THINK

I know a girl who is afraid of everything
Afraid of enjoying colourful spring
Afraid of fighting for her identity
Afraid of being judged by a hypothetical society

She is afraid of choosing her dream
Afraid of choosing her favourite stream
Afraid of speaking her heart out
Afraid of noisy violent shout

Afraid of all men of this world's
Afraid of leaving pain she holds
Afraid of flying so high
Afraid of painting her barren sky

Afraid of raising her voice against injustice
Afraid of telling truth to the police
Afraid of sharing her painful secrets
Afraid of making any stupid regrets

And one day metamorphosis happen just in an hour
When she meet her inner strength and superpower
She overcome all her painful fear and sadness white
Now she takes stand for all her right

FRIENDLY REMINDER

You are born to shine
Don't let anyone dim your inner sunshine

PERFECT DATE, TIME AND PLACE

What is the perfect date, time and place
For putting a glowing smile on your pale face
For celebrating your day-to-day victory
For creating an inspiring

What is the perfect date, time and place
For filling your darker lonely space
For painting your black and white dream
For adding chocolates of joy to your tasteless ice-cream

Is it New Year's Day
Or the playful Sunday
Or the first day of the month
Or happy December twenty fifth

Buddy you must not wait for a perfect day
Everyday is a God's gift and a special day
No matter if it is Tuesday at 4.25 pm
Or a smiling Monday at 5.15 am

You can do it right now
You can remodel it right now
When everything inside you whispers happily
I'm ready
I'm ready

FRIENDLY REMINDER

A friend is a cure for all the tension and stress
A reason behind the laughing happiness
A wind that brings positivity and joyousness
A diary that holds all the secrets and childness
A sweet home full of love and kindness

FRIENDSHIP ALWAYS REMAIN SAME

Some friends are close or some are miles apart from you
But the love between us is pure and true
They are always with us in sadness and blue
With them everyday we meet happiness new

Their happy vibes make our days bright
Their joyful calls light up our darker night
Their peaceful text calms our inner storm white
Their positivity makes everything alright

They never judge us for our imperfection
With them we never wear a mask of perfection
They never feel angry, jealousy and competition
They are a cure for all our stress and tension

No matter whenever true friends are close or so far
No matter whenever we see the sunrise or they see star
But like the sun and the moon, we complete each other
Our friendship always remains the same forever

FRIENDLY REMINDER

Just like the twinkling stars
Who never forget to shine bright
Buddy believes in yourselves
Even if there is a darker night

WE AS A CHILD

As a child we loved
The sun and the moon
We loved the shining stars
And count it every night's

As a child we loved orange candy
And share it with our friends too
We loved smiling rainbows
And smile back at them too

As a child we loved fairytales
And believed in lovely magic's
We loved beautiful nature
And take care as a valuable gift

As a child we were innocent and pure hearted
We only know to love unconditionally
We loved infinite things and laugh happily
Without needing any of them to love us back

FRIENDLY REMINDER

Buddy you are full of beauty
Love yourself happily

BEAUTY IS AN EMPATHY ATTITUDE

Beauty is an abstract art
Not a pictorial graph you see by eyes
Nor a rhyming sound you hear by ears
But a happy vibe that enlighten a heart

Beauty is an angelic smile
Not a materialistic thing you touched by hand
Nor a practical theory you proved by laws
But a calmness cloud that heals a painful wound

Beauty is an empathetic attitude
Not a glowing skin that wrinkled one day
Nor a pretty face turn old by age
But a kind heart which feels others pain

Beauty is an overwhelming joy
Not a shining fame you earned by your name
Nor a signature of your brand
But a helping soul which lifts other

Beauty is an inspiring thought
Not a physical parameter you explained by examples
Nor a checklist you always tried to fit in
But a positive light that ends darkness

FRIENDLY REMINDER

Holds those people close
Who makes you feel like a sunshine
In the darkness of blue raining night

STRANGER THAT CONNECTS TO MY HEART

When four walls caged me around
And playing the sad songs loud
Door invites me to come to the outside space
To find happiness in the crowd of an unknown face

The crowd of strangers take me to the city of India
Rome
The place which feels like a home
There is something special about these place
Where everyone heart is filled with love and kindness

I feel safe and reveal all my painful fears
That are buried inside my heart from many years
They support and remove my sadness blue
And promised, we are always with you

Their words give calmness to my inner storm
Their love again returns my lost glowing charm
They make me feel, I'm worthy
I'm a Rockstar and a shining glory

Now I find a place of my real happiness
Where there is a cure for every loneliness
Where stranger connects with my heart in a way forever
That no one known can ever

FRIENDLY REMINDER

Buddies
paint all the melancholy
in the colour of happiness
and let the whole world smiles
with you

I COULD PAINT MY WORLD

I could paint my night
With the dazzling rays of sunlight
Hoping the darkness end
In the colour of wind

I could paint my wall
With the whitish colours of snowball
Hoping the calmness comes again
In the comforting coldness of rain

I could paint my darker ways
With the smiling beam of golden rays
Hoping the whole world Enlight
In the glory of pinkish daylight

I could paint my scars
With the silvery colour of twinkling stars
Hoping the clouds sing
In the beauty of spring

I could paint my blue moon
With the happiness of red noon
Hoping the whole sky glow
In the gladness of singing snow

I could paint my night
With the dazzling rays of sunlight

FRIENDLY REMINDER

Maybe you just be happy for the small things
Like reading your favourite books in April noon
Or laughing so hard while talking to your friends
Or listening Shreya Ghoshal songs in calming evening
Maybe that's all that is really enough at the end of the
day

WHAT IF YOUR PINKISH SKY TURNS BLUE

What if your pinkish sky turns blue?
What if the Magical moon stop smiling at you?
What if there is no dazzling light in days?
Would the smiling sunshine on your face remains same
or change?

What if the blissful sun stops shining?
What if the angelic stars stop twinkling?
What if fairy cotton clouds stop raining?
What if your happy poems stop rhyming?
Would you cry so hard or you still smiling?

What if your world turns grey and blue?
What if the person you trust is not so true?
What if the blowing wind is not kind to you?
What if your windows don't show any happy view ?
Is your angelic eye still dare to see dreams new?

I know the sunshine on your face always smiles in
joyness
Your dreamy eyes always see the light of happiness
Because your heart is full of positivity, hope and
childness
You have a superpower to light up the darkness

FRIENDLY REMINDER

How strange
to wait for someone to make you happy
when your power house of happiness is right within you
when your happiness is you

EVERYDAY SMILE BRIGHT

Why are you finding yourself frail
Why are you always blaming yourself girl
Why don't you understand how precious you are
Why don't you see how beautiful you are

I know sometimes difficulties knock on your door
Sometimes you feel less happy, sad more
Sometimes clouds of negativity come through the
window
Sometimes you feel fear from your
own shadow

But buddy see you overcome all your sadness
And still trying to paint your life in happiness
Don't you think, you are strongest
Don't you think, you are the best

So stop crying over the life hurdles
Stop giving up on life's struggles
So everyday just stop for a while
And wear your cute charming smile

FRIENDLY REMINDER

And some stories never end
It continues and continues and continues
Because it's written with the ink of
love and happiness

WE DESERVES TRUE LOVE

We all deserve the one who will forever stay
The one who loves you every single day
No matter it's playful Sunday
Or chilling morning Monday

The one who loves you with all your imperfection
With them you never wear a mask of perfection
The one who disappears all your pain
With them you love dancing in the rain

The one who gives you wings to fly
The one who paints your darker sky
The one who supports to achieve your dream high
With them all your sadness says goodbye

The one who feels you like a home
The one who swipe away all your loneliness syndrome
The one who fills your darker empty space
The one who put a smile on your sad face

The one who never gets bored of you
The one whose love is unconditional and true
The one who proves loving you is not so hard
With them your name smiles on your wedding card

FRIENDLY REMINDER

Stop living in your own shadow
Don't let the clouds of doubt and insecurities
Dim your inner smiling sunshine
It's time to take control

LET PEOPLE THINK YOU ARE WEIRD

Let people think you're fool and perfect
Wanna start writing a book, do it
Wanna start learning guitar, do it
Wanna start your YouTube channel, do it

Wanna start your new business, do it
Wanna start opening a dance school, do it
Wanna start your motivational blog, do it
Wanna start your makeup tutorial, do it
Wanna start painting your dreams, do it

Don't be afraid of your failure, just Smile
Don't be afraid they call you crazy, just Smile
Don't be afraid they call you immature,
just Smile
Don't be afraid of what they levelled you,
just Smile
Don't be afraid of what they think of you,
just Smile

Live life for your happiness, friend
Paint your life in your favourite colour, friend
Enjoy every moment on your life, friend
Because life comes around once, friend
Just go out and do whatever make you happy, friend

FRIENDLY REMINDER

And when you're too busy in visiting
The back pages of your book
You miss creating everything happy and beautiful
In the new pages lies in front of you

CHOOSE HEALING OVER PAIN

How charming the alluring dawn
How friendly the blowing wind brown
How peaceful the glowing starlight
How happy the days and night
When you choose healing over pain

How calming the laughing moon
How bubbly the singing noon
How kind the dancing clouds white
How beautiful the smiling rainbow bright
When you Choose healing over pain

How humble the rains of April
How pleasing the December cool
How supportive the stranger cities
How blissful the limitless skies
When you choose healing over pain

How colourful the joyful nature
How lively the playing creature
How inspiring the rhyming words
How divine the hopeful world's
When you choose healing over pain

FRIENDLY REMINDER

In the race of being perfect and superior
Love your craziness, uniqueness
imperfection and childness

IMPERFECTLY PERFECT

In the crowd full of perfection
I just enjoyed my imperfection
No rooms for sadness and pain
I love dancing in happiness rain

In a world full of competition
I tried to find a magical solution
No space for jealousy, anger and race
Happy to see smiles on everyone's face

In the night full of darkness
I light up the lamp of kindness
No doors open for sadness and fear
I fix the blissful happy stars near

In the path full of black cloud
I enlighten the way by singing aloud
No windows open for thunderstorms voice
I have a million of reasons to rejoice

Everyone is special just the way they are
Like a delicious icecream chocobar
Everyone is imperfectly perfect
Try to understand perfection theories correct

FRIENDLY REMINDER

Buddies, be the kind of vibes that
heals the broken heart
And brings positivity and gladness

IT STARTED WITH A TEXT

It started with a text
I remembered I put a sad status about my ex
You replied are you ok or best
Or waiting for someone next

Instead of asking are you alright or broke
You just cracked a silly joke
Your healing words work as a chilling snowflake
And started healing my painful crack

We are insta friend from December nine
But our friendly bond start creating on November one
Our friendship is like the moon and sunshine
You make my days brighter and fine

You wiped my tears when I cry
You give me hopes to dream high
You are my cute charming sky
You give me wings of courage to fly

Thanks for making my day bright
Thanks for being my shining star in lonely night
Thanks for making my world happy and alright
Thanks for being my best friend and happiness light

FRIENDLY REMINDER

Buddies dares to live happily
In the world full of melancholy

SHE BELONGS TO THE HAPPY WORLD

She belongs to the world of light
Where angelic moon radiates blissful light
Where colourful rainbow smiles in golden light
Where magical stars dance on silvery moonlight

She lives happily in this chaotic world
She found peace in her poetic world
Her words fly happily in this pinkish world
And plant seeds of happiness in this lonely world

She plays the songs of happiness
In the room full of laughing happiness
She opens the window of happiness
Her wall is painted in the colour of happiness

She is like the song of hope
The one which give hopeless the glowing hope
The one which fills the heart with the joy of hope
The one which give dreamless a wing of hope

FRIENDLY REMINDER

Buddies
the time, world, season change
But the love of mothers remains unchanged

MOTHER'S LOVE NEVER CHANGES

Even if twinkling stars
Stopped shining at night
Even if the blissful moon
Stopped smiling in your dream
Even if the fairy cotton clouds
Have no longer pearls for rain
The love of mother
Will still remain the same
Caring, blissful and supportive

Even if the dazzling sun
Stopped laughing at days
Even if the delightful earth
Stopped rotating at its axis
Even if the charming rainbows
Have no longer colours for sky blue
The love of a mother
Will still remain the same
Unconditional, pure and divine

FRIENDLY REMINDER

The world is filled with words and rhymes
Still, we don't choose happy words to heal
a crying heart

RECIPE OF HAPPY POEM

Fill these blank page
With life lessons of every stage
Wrote some magical words
Which inspires this beautiful world's

Make sure the words you wrote
Transform into a positive quote
Make sure the lesson you taught
Transfer into a positive thought

Add some beautiful prose
So that your words smell like a rose
Add some sugar to it
So that your poetry tasted sweet

Paint your words with happy emotion
That always gives a friendly solution
Enlightened your blissful ideas
With the colourful Diwali diya's

Give a hopeful title
Which give strength to win every battle
At last mention your shining name
Which gives everyone a glowing fame

FRIENDLY REMINDER

Do you know what's really cool
Loving your true self without any filters
and edit

BE HAPPY EVEYTIME

When you are happy the way you look
When you are happy the way you live
When you are happy with a dimple on your face
When you are happy with the things you have
You will experience true happiness forever

When you start embracing your scars
When you start accepting your imperfection
When you start focusing on the positive sides
When you start smiling while looking at the stars
You will experience true happiness forever

When you stop comparing yourself to others
When you stop fitting in other's expectations
When you stop putting your happiness into another
hands
When you don't beg someone to love you
You will experience true happiness forever

When you start following your passion
When you enjoy your crazy childness
When you start loving yourself first
When you believe you are worthy of all good things
You will experience true happiness forever

FRIENDLY REMINDER

And the one who stole the happy stars
From your blissful sky
Can never be your golden sunshine

I LOVE YOU SINCE DAY NINE

I love you since the day nine
But your happy sky never be mine
You promised me our love remains same till the end
But always leave my hand in front of your friend

You ignored me every single day
You controlled me all the way
Stupid me, who think our love is like
shore and sea
It's me who fool myself that you loved me

It hurts when you compare my look
It hurts when you say, I'm like a boring book
It hurts when you didn't make any effort
It hurts when you didn't support

You know true love is all about supporting each other
Loving, Caring, and uplifting each other
True love didn't care about how beautiful you are
They love you for who you are

It takes me four years to realize
You are no longer be bright star of my happy skies
Now, it's high time to let you go and say goodbye
Because some goodbye is good for your
mental peace and happiness high

FRIENDLY REMINDER

Buddies
Stop hating yourself for everything you
"don't have"
Start loving yourself for everything you
"have"

A LETTER TO HOPE

Dear hope,
Thank you for always smile beside me
When I don't have clear vision to see
When I don't find any way of happiness
Your blissful rays act as a source of joyness

Thank you for making me to see the light
When I don't have any shining stars bright
When I don't hear my inner voice
Your bold vibes mute the outer stormy noise

Thank you for lifting me up
When I finally decided to give up
When I don't have any courage to try
Your smiling blanket act as an inspiring sky

Thanks for walking with me in the dark
When my days turn blue and black
When I don't have any evening fine
You are being my peaceful sunshine

Thanks for showing me my real beauty
When I forgot my true identity
When my blissful moon is half
Your motivation makes me laugh

Thank you for always smile beside me
When I don't have clear vision to see

FRIENDLY REMINDER

We live a life for mere reputation
Change ourselves to fit in societal theory of perfection
Trying so hard to keep up what everyone tell
And trapped our happiness in a golden jail

LET'S MOVE TO OUR FAVORITE PLACE

Let's move to the place
Where sky is free from photochemical smog
Where there is no bluish fog

Let's move to the place
Where blowing wind is free from harmful pollutants
Where there are no dangerous mutants

Let's move to the place
Where blissful rain is free from damaging acid
Where drinking and smoking is still invalid

Let's move to the place
Where no agriculture land is sold to industrialist
Where kindness act as a universal catalyst

Let's move to the place
Where meadows still have singing sparrow
Where no one cry out in sorrow

Let's move to the place
Where biodiversity make you fall in wonder
Where abundance of matter gold, silver and copper

Let's move to our favourite place
Where childness dance carefree
Where happiness, love and blessings are free

FRIENDLY REMINDER

How can you be so
Hateful to yourself
When you tried your level best
Be proud of yourself

WHAT IF I WOULD'VE NEVER DARED TO FIGHT

What if
I would have never dared to speak out
For my right
For my happiness

I wouldn't have inhaled
The aroma of crimson positivity
From the blooming roses
Planted in the backyard of kindness garden

I wouldn't have dreamed
To become a world-famous novelist
Instead of being materialistic things
That only decorates a lonely home

I wouldn't have enjoyed
The freedom to fly high
And somehow like a caged bird
I'm trapped inside four walled jail

I wouldn't have tasted
The lovely sweetness of
The world famous Gulab-jamun
Of Delhi Bhagatram's sweets shop

I wouldn't have visualised
The colour of happiness
The glory of calmness
The beauty of success

WHAT IF I WOULD'VE NEVER DARED TO FIGHT

FRIENDLY REMINDER

You deserve a kind of love
Which takes away sadness, pain
and insecurities
And brings a lot of happiness, hope
and poetry

DOES THE LOVE REALLY COMPLICATED

Does the love really complicated
Like a tricky concepts of history world
Like the difficult problem of geometry
Like the concept of the Haber process of chemistry

The answer is too many
Different people, different story
Some say, love is suffering
Some say, no love stories have a happy ending

Maybe love isn't like everyone said
Maybe love is also misunderstand
Maybe we never give love a chance to explain
Maybe love is as simple as making a paper plane

Maybe love is simple like adding a teaspoon of sugar to
coffee
Maybe love is simple like singing your favourite song
carefree
Maybe love is as simple as smiling back in a reflective
mirror
Maybe love is as simple as counting number without
error

Maybe love is supporting each other in ups and downs
Maybe love is filling cream of happiness in tasteless
cupcakes
Maybe love is a hopeful song playing in the rain
Maybe love also wants to see as a pure true love again

FRIENDLY REMINDER

Wind of melancholy constantly try to uproot happiness
Not knowing that our roots of positivity run deep

SHE IS UNSTOPPABLE

She survived a painful war
That tells her darker scar
But she is a warrior who chooses happiness everyone
That proved her laughing rhyme

She cried out at night
That tells her pillow white
But she is a strong girl who walks with a smile everyday
That proved her happy day

She shared her secrets to the moon
That tells stars at noon
But she a fearless girl who chooses to shine
That proved her glowing face toward sunshine

She fights with the hypothetical society
That tells her unique identity
But she is a winner who wins every battle
That proved her inspiring book title

Yes, she is an ordinary girl
Just like us, like a girl in a dress purple
Who decided not to bend her knees
To the destructive storms and powerful difficulties

FRIENDLY REMINDER

Stop comparing yourself to others
Smiling sunflowers are pretty but so are
The night full of magical stars
And they look nothing alike

YOU ARE NOT YOUR AGE

You are not your age
Nor the colour of your eyes
You are not a face
Or a dimple on your smiling space

You are not your name
Nor the charm of your fame
You are not a height
Or a perfection of standard weight

You are the glow of your eyes
When you see stars in skies
You are the laughing of your world's
And the cuteness of your words

You are the smiles of your heart
And the inspiring poetry you wrote
You are the heart filled with kindness
And the favourite songs of happiness

You are made of so much beauty
But still you doubted about your identity
Buddy cherishes your cuteness
You are the crown of whole universe

FRIENDLY REMINDER

Be such a kind and happy hearted person
That heals every broken heart and melancholy season

DARE TO BE KIND HEARTED PERSON

Dare to be the one
Who can see the pain behind the bright smile
Who can feel the fear behind the brave voice
Who can hear the crying heart behind the laughing noise

Dare to be the one
Who can be everyone friends
Who can paint the sky with happy words
Who can add chocolate of joy in this lonely world's

Dare to be the one
Who can love themselves more
Who can prioritise their happiness first
Who can change their bad days into good ones

Dare to be the one
Who can wipe away all the sadness and pain
Who can heal every broken heart
Who can put a bright smile on a pale face

Dare to be the one
Who can make everyone laugh
Who can enlighten everyone's life
The one who is loved by everyone

DARE TO BE KIND HEARTED PERSON

FRIENDLY REMINDER

Buddies, we all have a magical power to rewrite our
golden life stories
With the happy ink of hope and courage

CALLING THE HAPPY GIRL BACK

I started calling that happy girl back
Whom I lost a few years ago
The girl who enjoys every moment simplest
The girl who makes everyone happiest

The girl who loves herself more
The girl who laughs every single day
The girl who follows her passion
The girl who is free from stress and tension

I started composing inspiring poetries again
I started writing supportive letters to myself
I started playing with kids
I started making new friends

Hoping she would come out
With a bright familiar smile
And happily, says, hello beautiful
Let's start again making your life colourful

Because I knew
She is within me
She only needs self-love, courage and gratitude
To come again to the outside world again

FRIENDLY REMINDER

Paint your black and white life canvas
With the laughing colour of childness

I LOVE THE TWINKLING STARS

I love these magical stars
It reminds me of the day, when my world is free of scars
The day when fairies came into my dream
When this sky is cute pinkish cream

The day when everyone is my friend
When my kiddish talk have no end
The day when I'm the happiest person in this universe
When my life is like a playful happy verse
But then days by days all my happiness gone

All days my thoughts are revolving around
Money, competition and gold
In the race of bluish victory
I lost my pinkish happy glory

I have a big car, money and lots of bank balance
But what I missed most is my childhood happiness
I learned a beautiful lesson from the skies
Never says your inner child goodbye

Now buddies just stop for a while
And look at the moon and smile
Let your thoughts be laughing and wild
Let again be a happy child

FRIENDLY REMINDER

And the way you paint your life
with happiness and self-love is itself
the greatest superpower
Keep doing buddy

MY DREAM WORLD

I dream a world where
No one is sad
Where love rules
And positivity inspires

I dream a world where
There is no place for discrimination
Where humanity is religion
And truth is prayers

I dream a world where
There is no hatred
Where life is full of blessings
And happiness is everywhere

I dream a world where
There is no stress
Where love enlighten the earth
Where happy stars paint black and white dreams

I dream a world where
No impurities can pollute the soul
Where flowers fill the heart with beauty
And the moon carrier sadness away

I dream a world where
No one is sad

FRIENDLY REMINDER

Fairytales come true
When true love is with you

LOVE IN TWENTY TWENTY FIVE

It is twenty twenty five
And falling in love is hard and matching vibe
Not because people don't fall in love at a moment
But because they afraid of commitment

This is an era of heartache
Where love is less, more heartbreak
Where calmness is less, more stress
Where happiness is less, more sadness

The era where love come with a gift of pain
Where lovers cry in the sadness rain
The era where true love is hard to find
Where the blowing wind is not so kind

But apart from all these blue
True live is waiting for me and you
And trust me Buddy, true love finds you one day
Just like chilling winter find sunray

FRIENDLY REMINDER

Day dreaming of being a queen
with billions of kingdoms is maybe
More alluring version than Caring
what 7.8 billion people think

YOU ARE NOT WHAT OTHERS THINK

You are not what others think
You are the sunrise you love to watch
The blooming smiling flowers
And the happy poems you wrote

You are not the scars on your body
Or pimples on your face
You are not the colour of your skin or body weight
You are the favourite books you read everyday

You are not insecurities of your heart
You are the peaceful clouds that brings calmness
You are not the fear of failure
You are the blissful sunshine that enlight darkness

You are not the imperfection of life
You are the hopeful songs and colourful childness
You are not what others think
You are what you love

FRIENDLY REMINDER

Buddies
all your sadness, agony and
depression will end
When you keep positivity, happiness and
hope as your best friend

SEEK JOY SIMPLEST MOMENT

Seek a joy in the moment simplest
Enjoy your life to the fullest
From your busy schedule take some break
Forgot all your past mistake

Write a poem that rhyme
Spend alone some me time
Wake up and go on a morning walk
Call your friends while following rule walk and talk

Laugh like an adorable child
Let your thoughts be peaceful and kind
Forgive the people who do something wrong
You know you're so so strong

Don't run behind the race of perfection
Fall in love with your childness and imperfection
You're like a playful charming verse
You deserve all the happiness of universe

FRIENDLY REMINDER

We are all heroes. We are all villains. We are all kind. We are all rude. We are all beautiful. We are all dull. It just depends on who wrote the story

PUT A LEVEL OF GLADNESS ON YOU

When you speak a lot, they say you are dramatic
When you speak less, they say you are diplomatic
When you laugh a lot, they say you are crazy
When you laugh a less, they say you are cringe
No matter what, they always put a level on you
But when you know you are worthy, you are sunshine
true
You put a level of happiness, sweet and loving on you

When you enjoy a lot, they say you are mad
When you enjoy less, they say you are weird
When you're courageous a lot, they say you are rude
When you're courageous less, they say you are cloud
brown
No matter what, they always tried to put you down
But when you know you are valuable, you're diamond
pure
You put a level of bravery , kind and cute on you

When you're ambitious a lot, they say you are showing
off
When you're ambitious less, they say you are tough
When you motivated a lot, they you are overconfident
When you motivated less, they say you are ignorant
No matter what, they always stab on your back
But when you know you are intelligent, you are beautiful
You put a level of bright, optimistic and cheerful on you

FRIENDLY REMINDER

And Buddies, it's so unkind of you
To be unkind of yourself
Don't you know you are a blissful sunshine
Your glow makes everyone smile
Call yourself pretty name

A MEETING WITH MY OLDER VERSION

Today when the sun is on the horizon
I meet my olden version
I realized people that left me
Were telling a big lie

It was a lie that I'm weak
Because I have a superpower to shine in the dark
It was a lie that I'm broken
I can rebuild myself from the broken pieces again

I was a lie that I'm ugly
I can see a girl in the mirror smiles happily
It was a lie that I'm a loser
I achieved my dream and proved myself
a winner

It was a lie that I'm full of stupidity
I'm a confident girl dealing with everything maturely
It was a lie that I will always be a survivor
I'm a brave girl and a life saviour

Everything was a lie and lie
Which was said by them and judgement society
I'm a gem, I'm perfect
I'm worthy, I'm important

FRIENDLY REMINDER

You have power to create a happiness you
'Search'
Read it again

CREATE YOUR OWN HAPPINESS

When the weather is not in your favour
When sky is not painted in your favourite colour
When the courageous stars aren't so so bold
When your cold coffee isn't so so cold
Definitely this rushed, but then you might
try smiling

When the evening moon is not so so charming
When your afternoon winter is not so so warming
When the singing wind is not so so kindly
When your relatives are not so so friendly
Surely this rushed, but then you might
try smiling

When the dancing clouds is not so so white
When your morning new is not so so bright
When the outside world not so so calming
When your poetry is not in rhyming
Definitely this rushed, but then you might
try smiling

Smile have a power to change the world
Smile have an antidote for all the wound
When you smile everyday and keep smiling
Life always smiles back at you
So keep smiling and smiling
Smiling and smiling

THANK YOU